D1556448

NOTES FROM THE
NERVOUS BREAKDOWN LANE

NOTES FROM THE
NERVOUS BREAKDOWN LANE

CARTOONS BY
KEN BROWN

PERENNIAL LIBRARY

Harper & Row, Publishers, New York
Cambridge, Philadelphia, San Francisco,
London, Mexico City, São Paulo, Singapore, Sydney

To Lisa

NOTES FROM THE NERVOUS BREAKDOWN LANE. Copyright © 1985 by Kenneth M. Brown. All rights reserved. Printed in the United States of America. No part of this book may be used or reproduced in any manner whatsoever without written permission except in the case of brief quotations embodied in critical articles and reviews. For information address Harper & Row, Publishers, Inc., 10 East 53rd Street, New York, N.Y. 10022. Published simultaneously in Canada by Fitzhenry & Whiteside Limited, Toronto.

Library of Congress Cataloging-in-Publication Data

Brown, Ken.
    Notes from the nervous breakdown lane.

    1. American wit and humor, Pictorial. I. Title.
NC1429.B8514A4   1985   741.5'973   85-42733
ISBN 0-06-096014-0 (pbk.)

MARGE 'N' AL PONDER A POT ROAST

A 17' TOASTER OVEN, WASHED ASHORE AT WELLFLEET, MASS.

THE MOON MUST BE IN KLUTZ

THE DANCE OF THE MALADROIT ACCOUNTANTS

BOLO CROSSING

NEUROTRANSMITTERS TAKE A HOLIDAY

THE SEA GOD TANGAROA GIVES BIRTH TO GODS AND MEN ON THE ROBINSONS' RUG

GRANNY CALLED ATTENTION TO HER NEW RED WEDGIES

**OUR LADY OF THE LARGE ZUCCHINI
AT THE BLESSING OF THE ZUKES**

STEVE AND IDI

GEORGE AND MARTHA

INDOLENCE ON PARADE

TOURNAMENT OF TWINKIES, PASADENA

LIVING WITH THE BOMB

DON AND HELEN DROP BY FOR DIP

HAVE A NICE DAY

NO FRIES ON ME

FRANK AND HANK RETURN FROM THE HUNT

THE TOASTER BOOSTER CLUB

THE CAT DRAGGED INN, AN OLD LANDMARK, ATLANTIC CITY, N.J.

HOME OF ED PARKER

INTERNATIONAL HOUSE OF CARBOHYDRATES

LOCAL VIEWS by Ken Brown

DINO-RAMA

OUR LADY OF THE UNIROYAL

LET'S FRY UP THESE SUCKERS

MALCOLM LOCATED THE MISSING MOLLUSK

CABIN FEVER

TALENT NIGHT AT THE MITCHELLS

BRIDAL PROCESSION WITH LARGE LIME JELL-O, LITHUANIA

BRATWURST BROADJUMP, BERLIN

EASTER ISLAND, BUSINESS ROUTE

PUT UP THE TOP, POP

PORTRAIT OF A HAPPY FAMILY

DARYL HAD DIFFICULTY RELATING TO DAD

LAKE FLACCID

WOLFMAN AMADEUS MOZART

VELCRO-BEARING TROUT—LAKE AGOGAGOG, VT.

LIVING WITH THE BOMB

SPOT BREAKS

SUMMERTIME, AND THE LIVING IS CRAZY

GREETINGS FROM MONDAY MORNING

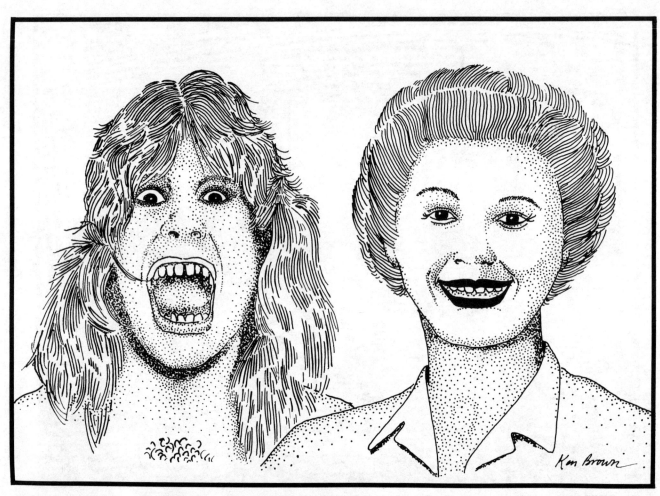

OZZIE AND HARRIET

IKE AND TINA

FRANK'S FROG COULD SNAG FRIES FROM FOUR FEET

TORO, TORO, TORO MEET THE LAWN NYMPHS OF NYACK, N.Y.

FRANK AND PHYLLIS AMUSED THEMSELVES FOR HOURS WITH THEIR CHINESE FINGER TRAP

ART LINKLETTER ROCK

HALL OF PHLEGM

GREETINGS FROM THE GREAT OUTDOORS

I CAN'T SEEM TO FALL ASLEEP WITHOUT THE SOUND OF
BOTTLES BREAKING ON PAVEMENT

PRECISION DONUT DRILL

PRECISION JELL-O DRILL TEAM

PRECISION TWINKIE FLIPPING

FORM AND FOOD

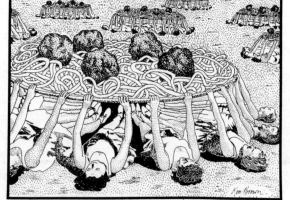

PRECISION PASTA PRESS

LIVING WITH THE BOMB

LIFESTYLES OF THE RANK AND FERAL

SONNY BONO AT THE 8:10 EXPRESS

PIA ZADORA AT EASTER ISLAND

CHARO AT CADILLAC RANCH

ED McMAHON AT STONEHENGE

CELEBS TRY TO MOVE LARGE IMMOBILE OBJECTS ON **THAT'S IMMOVABLE!**

THE JAVA MAINTENANCE CLINIC

MIDGE MARVELED AT TED'S TELEKINETIC TALENTS

ONCE AGAIN, DIRK DAZZLED THEM WITH HIS DEXTERITY

ANOTHER SATISFIED CUSTOMER AT BIG RED'S ROUTE 1 CHILI RANCH

AVENUE OF THE LAVA LAMPS

GREETINGS FROM THE FRAY

SPEAK SOFTLY AND WEAR A LOUD SHIRT

RECKLESS ABANDON

THE OUT-OF-CONTROL TOWER

MR. MUFFLER RUNS AMOK

SKINHEADS IN THE ROCKIES

THE TROPIC OF TORPOR

WHITE MEN IN TIES DISCUSSING MISSILE SIZE

SOME DAY SON, ALL THIS . . .

SPOTLIGHT ON DAY-OLD MEATLOAF

FRIES SWIMMING UPSTREAM TO SPAWN

SOUP DE VILLE

TWINKIE TOSS, TENAFLY, N.J.

THE WORLD'S BIGGEST BALL OF TOASTER OVENS

BERNICE AND BOB ENTER THE TORRID ZONE

THE KIND OF CROISSANTS THEY GROW HERE

LIVING WITH THE BOMB

REMEMBER WHEN WE WERE KIDS
AND WOULD DANGLE OUR HANDS
OVER THE SIDE OF THE BED...

THEN PULL THEM UP JUST BEFORE
ANY OF THOSE WEIRD CREATURES
THAT HUNG OUT DOWN THERE
COULD GET AT THEM?

COOL JERKS

DON'T BE SO GLUM, CHUM

WHISTLER'S BROTHER ERNIE FROM DULUTH

WOLFMAN JACKSON POLLOCK

POPE-ALOPE

MICKEY MAO

ON WEEKENDS, MRS. TRIMBLEY PICKS UP GROCERY MONEY AS THE HUMAN CANNONBALL

THE WINDOW OF VULNERABILITY

LOYOLA RENOUNCES THE WORLD

THE ECSTASY OF SPOT

FOR HIS FINAL ACT, ROLAND TURNED TO DUST

MP12Q